Fluent in Rivers

~

KATHLEEN BREWIN LEWIS

FUTURECYCLE PRESS
www.futurecycle.org

Published by FutureCycle Press
Lexington, Kentucky, USA

ISBN 978-1-938853-64-7

For my dearly beloveds:
Jeff, Ben, Rosalee, Mama—
and in memory of my father

Contents

Acknowledgments

If I opened my arms I could hear

Every shell in the sea find the word
It has tried to put into my mouth.

—James Dickey, *Drowning With Others*

Eventually, all things merge into one...

—Norman Maclean, *A River Runs Through It*

Whereupon the Writer Thinks
She Is the Center of the Universe

In a lonely corner of the night,
she sits writing at the kitchen table
while her house sleeps. The outside
is trying to come in.

Dusty moths and brown beetles
are beating on the glass,
covering the window panes
with their soft wings and crisp bodies,
drawn to, absolutely craving,
her light.

She is spooked, distracted;
she is finally flattered,
writing more intently
for her fluttering audience,
strangely moved by the staccato
of their gentle collisions.

This night is alive, she is thinking,
it is pulsing with the beat of my heart.
And all eyes—
all of the tiny, glittering eyes—
are on me.

Eggshell

The morning is a chiffon scarf. A child
steps out into soft light,
a spotted egg cupped in his hands.
I rest my palm on the place where
his bowed head meets his slim neck.
Sometimes this is prophecy,
sometimes recollection.
To touch him this way is always a blessing.

Afternoon, a chambray shirt, rolls its sleeves up.
The boy lifts his head, tells me
of his dreaming, turns his attention
to the plunge of a red-tailed hawk.
There is composure in his turning.
His shoulders broaden; he grows taller than I.
The egg cracks open. The night is a winter
coat with silver buttons.

Fluent in Rivers

Before you knew me,
before I came to root myself
in these red clay hills beside your father,
I lived by the coastline,
        swam its creeks and rivers.

Afloat in brackishness,
watching blue crabs pedal
sideways and away,
I heard the cry of the marsh hen,
        was solitary but never afraid.

Shoulders draped with dark water,
I let cool tendrils of current
carry me around the bend
until I turned, kicked, stroked my way back
        to the sunburnt dock, the anchor of its ladder.

The clacking of grizzled oyster beds,
white heron lifting over green marsh,
fish leaping like celebrants,
the suck and seep of tidal life,
        holding my breath, gliding through all.

Today the wind moans around the house,
rattles the cellar door. I peel potatoes
while you sleep in the back bedroom.
When you wake, I need to tell you:
        Before you knew me,
        before I was your mother,
        I swam through summer,
        was fluent in rivers.

This Lonely Cognizance

He has hiked deep into the woods
and told himself
he will not leave
until he has his answer,
and on that first night
he cannot sleep for listening.
The insects, the stirrings
in the dry leaves,
the yowl of the coyote.
One snap of one twig
and he almost shouts: *Who's there?*
At first light he shuts his eyes
and when he wakes mid-morning
vows to keep a fire burning
through the sullen night.
He spends the afternoon gathering
downed branches, broken limbs.
When the darkness returns,
he is ready, has layered
his wood pile properly,
strikes a match on the sole of his boot.
At first he is pragmatic,
places potatoes on the fire,
sets an open can of soup at the edge.
His thoughts turn to the Lakota,
their sweat lodges, the desire he feels
for revelation, a splintering of the self
into these billion stars, reassembly
as a better man, transfused, refined,
steady as this great gray mountain.

As the night deepens, he adds wood
to the fire, lets the pungent smoke saturate
his hair, lungs, dizzying him until
the crack and pop of the ashing logs
rouse his heart, incite a vision:
    a solitary man beside a campfire,
            face illumined by orange glow,
            viewed from a great distance,
            seeing himself   being seen,
        watched over, watching,
                acknowledged surely   and he thinks
            this is his answer, this seeing
        and being seen, this knowing,
which seems enough.
In the morning
he will pack his few things.

Voracity

I want to know
the common names
of growing things—
ferns, oaks, thistles,
sumac, lilies—then I want
to break into their hearts,
slit their stems with my thumbnail,
peel bark, splinter twigs,
place spores, pollen, pith, phloem
on my tongue's tip,
swallow sap.   Crack
the botanic bones
of this evergreen world,
pry ripe marrow—
    and I will
renounce the trail,
go deeper into woods,
stand in thick rain to do it.

Dogwood Winter

Three days after Easter
and the temperature
has slipped, fallen.

Flakes of flowering cherry
swirl with pale petals
of unseasonable snow.

A bald yellow egg
from the weekend's hunt
lies unfound on the bitter ground.

We pull our sweaters
tight around us, hope
the hyacinths won't freeze, wait

for spring to strong-arm winter,
roll it back
where it belongs.

Bliss

I'm not exactly certain
what circadian rhythms are,
not really sure I want to know,
content to love the sound of them,
to imagine what they might be:
Celadon moth circling
rusty porch light, pair of mallards
asleep on black pond, ocean's
swell and sweep of shore,
crash diets of the moon.

A dictionary could end
the mystery, lift the veil
separating fantasy from fact.

I would rather
keep picturing:
a striped feather
scything the air,
graceful dances
between man and beast,
the planets afloat
in a susurrant place,
honeybees droning
deep
in bright blossoms.

On the Brink

—Island in the Sky, Canyonlands National Park

I would swear this is where Christ
spent his forty days and nights,
parched, starved, on the brink.

What tempts me as I stand here,
something like hunger
gnawing my long bones?
I have tried turning stones into bread,
and though the urge to jump lurks,
I will not do it.

I am drawn to descend, walk down
into the sheer silence, become
a speck moving between
sunbaked rocks and hard places
toward a remnant river.

I want to know what would find me first:
rattlesnake or ranger,
heatstroke or angel,
fiend or god.

Collusion on the Middle Provo

He knows it is my first time
so he is patient, leading me
down the path to the riverbed,
through meadows of red clover,
lamb's ears, saffron yarrow.

He stands me amid the stones
in the river's rush, places
the rod in my hand, covers
my hand with his, talks of technique:
how to cast, mend, hook, reel.
And so I unfurl, over and over again,
until I feel what he means:
the tug and tear of a fish on the line.

Let the line run when the fish jerks,
he coaches. *Reel it smoothly in as the fish tires.*
And when the trout rises, he laughs,
congratulates me, scoops
my fish into his net,
tells me I'm a natural.

He says to wet my hands
in the bracing current, then cup them
while he unhooks, lifts, puts the trout
in touch with me.

I want to press my lips to her,
she is so marvelous, pulsing, sleek
against my palms; instead I bend
and whisper, so he can't hear me,

that I'm sorry for hurting her
and I wish her well.

I turn my back to him,
lower her into the glistening river
that snatches, bears her away.

Good Friday, Tybee Island

The sun throbs, bleeds down sky,
soaks into the Back River and its marsh.
It halves, slivers, then it is finished,
leaving the air softer,
sadder than before.

Silhouettes cross roseate sky;
brown pelicans come to catch their dinner.
They plunge, one by one, for a fish—
tiny, vacillating, silver—spied from on high
in the gloaming.

Can you see me,
standing on this pier as darkness swells?
Do you hunger for me, as I for you?
Do you mean, at the end of the day,
to fish me out of deep water, to take me,
take me as I am?

Re-turning

I have been gone from here long enough
to startle at the sight of seagulls
in the Publix parking lot
where I have come to collect
my mother's prescriptions.
They strut the asphalt, circle
the cart return. Their cries
set off a spinning in my head.
I dislocate the day, recall salt water.
At the center of this gyre:
my father and me,
on the beach building drip castles,
hands curved into birds' beaks,
sand liquescent dribbling
through our fingers. The sea
flings sheets upon the shore.

The Husker

When it comes to shucking, she's insatiable,
pulling back the stiff green leaves, listening hungrily
to the rasp and rip. She consumes herself
with the stripping, snaps off the stump, plucks
each clingy strand of the tassel. Then she rubs
her index finger over the rows of bulging kernels
as if they were braille or pearls or little teeth,
piles the yellow spikes tenderly
into the crisper of her fridge.

To justify her habit, she concocts fresh corn salads
with red onion, cider vinegar, torn basil,
a little salt, or sautés the bright kernels in olive oil
with shrimp and diced tomatoes. Her husband sighs
at the frequency of these dishes. When they make love,
she conjures the sound of the husking,
strokes her cheek with a lock of corn silk
after he rolls over, falls asleep.

She dreams of walking
through acres of summer cornfields,
tables loaded with brimming bushels
just waiting for her touch.
All that tightly guarded ripeness!
The saddest thing she can think of
is the colorless silence of the gnawed cob.

Coyote

There you are, standing by my swimming pool.
I've never seen you before, but I know who you are.
You're more handsome than I've been led to believe.
Your presence explains the missing cat signs
around the neighborhood, why I never see
brown bunnies on the lawn anymore.
And all the while I've been watching you,
you've never taken your golden eyes
off of me. I am the one who finally looks away.

Autobiography

Your first knowledge, the nooks and crannies
of your parents' bodies: crooks of their arms,
scent of their necks, your head resting
between their breasts and collarbones.

Your first loves, the small, soft things—
feathers, young animals, blushing puffs of bloom
from the mimosa tree. Start to collect
the harder things: stones, sticks, shells—
pockets and pails of them. Treasures.

Become graceful. Enter the water,
begin to swim. Dance unashamed, arms wide.
Legs pump the creaking swing,
arc against the sky.

Learn to pay your respects: climb trees,
discover, but do not touch, birds' nests.
Study the contents of the tidal pool—
sand dollar, sea olive, translucent crab.
Smell the poppy; do not pick it.
Resolve to break nothing.

Trespass

On the trail to the ruined textile mill, the wild azaleas
are in bloom, the magnolia thick with fat white buds.

I mean to set my mantle of care down beside
this stony creek, hide it among the hardwoods.

Each step is a lightening, the sound of water
flowing over rocks a mercy.

After a mile or more, the Civil War relic comes into view,
banked and boarded beside the shoals.

There's a breach in the old bricks, and I step through
into the dim and dusty quiet.

A rustling in the eaves, small shower of leaves.
Doves or pigeons, I imagine, or a snug nest of squirrels.

Instead, a length of black rope falls from the rafters,
thuds on the ground, slithers into a dark corner.

I shiver, slip back where I came from—
into the day, the spring, this world.

The Largesse of Morning

Wake up slender
to faint light
seeping through shutters.

The sun, a freshly peeled orange,
begins its climb;
dawn spreads out a picnic
on bright cloth.

Breakfast on melon, egg, hope—
grant yourself
reprieve from disbelieving.
Breathe the aroma
of exonerated earth.

The day is bound to narrow.
Its conclusion
promises to be dark.
For now, the world
is filling with radiance.
See how the morning glories
trumpet on the white fence!

Sweater Weather

Disrobing trees, woolly clouds.
A thin creek stitches itself
into the red valley.
You want to be warmer.
A skein of geese pulls
across the afternoon sky.

Order Lepidoptera, Family Papilionoidea

He loves them for their colors, the silence of their flight,
their fragility, which is something like his own.
His room is filled with cases of their splayed beauty.
He's told himself the creatures were found lying
on soft paths at the end of their life cycles.
He can't believe they were caught to be pinned down.

He studies his field guide, strives to learn the Latin:
Vanessa atalanta, Thymelicus silvestris, Inachis io.
He's already memorized the common names
that reflect their hues—Clouded Yellow, Purple Hairstreak,
Mazarine Blue.

Mother is a butterfly, he thinks. She knows how
to touch him lightly in ways he can bear. Sometimes
she tells him she needs to hug him, would he be brave
for a few seconds and let her hold him gently? He would.
Mother smells like lilies. Father shakes his hand too hard.

He's promised to sit at the table, have Thanksgiving dinner
with the family, *try very, very hard* to make conversation
with his cousins. *Earth to Jonathan!* his little brother trumpets,
when he doesn't realize Aunt Beryl is trying to pass him
the sweet potatoes. Everyone together is so noisy.
Sister lays two fingers on his knee, which calms him.
He wonders if she is training to be a mother.

He answers a question from his uncle, remembers
to make eye contact, eats the food on his plate

in his usual clockwise fashion. Then he notices the centerpiece,
a hollowed-out pumpkin filled with flowers, thinks
how the mums are the color of the Sooty Copper,
has to excuse himself from the table, return to his room
full of bright and delicate wings.

Aubade in a Time of Rain

All night it fell,
falls still, and so

there will be no blushing
by the sky this morning,

no wisps of young light
to slip through the shutters,

coax our eyes open; and yet
you wake,

as if it were any other day,
stir, turn toward me

amid the gray thrumming
to tender the embrace

that comes, I now know,
in rain or shine.

There are days

you scrounge the last onion
from the dry field,
bruise a heel
on some stone from the river,
rake a serrated elm leaf
across your blue wrist.
This is not one of those days.

This is a day
you lace your fingers
into thick grass,
rouse yourself
with a sense of belonging,
tread so lightly on sandy soil,
you leave a tender imprint.

Dovetail these:
sprout of radish,
call of nuthatch,
flight of dragonfly,
whiff of rain. Snap
a forked branch
from the hazel tree;
divine the source
of this day.

Landscape with River Birch

There is no river here,
just a gunite swimming pool.
You were planted for your bark,
crispy curls of taupe, cinnamon, cream.
But you grew too tall, forked over the roof,
cast the climbing roses into shade.

He resolved to remove your offending limb,
stanch the shower of leaves
that threatened to clog the gutter,
allow more sun to fall
on his odorless buds.

I bought him a book about pruning,
told him it mattered how and when
a tree was cut. He didn't want a book,
was mad to use his ladder and saw,
wouldn't wait for summer
when your sap would slow.
He pulled the saw teeth back and forth
until he severed one of your arms.

The pruning book warned
that river birches are *bleeders,*
shouldn't be cut in spring
when their juices freely flow. For days

you've been weeping without ceasing,
sap pooling on the driveway, a little lake.
The drops spatter when they land.

I stand in the drip,
look up at your wound,
let the tears fall on my face.

Whole, Wide World

Heat rises from asphalt in corrugations;
flecks of rainbow snag the skeins
of oscillating sprinklers. Unseen bird
in the palmetto next door
repeats a two-beat trill
punctual as a heartbeat.

Vacant seashell cupped to the ear
will surely sound like a faraway ocean.
Fragrant earth beneath the feet
undulates, emits a fulsome vibrato.

Everything aquiver, everything wavering—
this waterfall world inclines
so voluptuously toward the light.

Sapelo

*—In the 1850s, 385 slaves lived and toiled
on this Georgia barrier island.*

This sultry place, built
on the bare backs of slaves:
malarial rice fields, shell-studded
tabby structures, cane and cotton
plantations, solitary lighthouse. All

ruins now, but for the lighthouse—
rebuilt, relit, in a better century.
A ninth generation ferries the sound
to weekday work on the mainland,
digs Saturday clams and oysters
from deep mud at low tide. Still

the island mourns.
Its twisted oaks wear
shrouds of Spanish moss,
bear boughs heavy
with resurrection fern. Thick

rattlesnakes drape and sun
on the planter's headstone.

Camellias

—*for Lafe*

French doors open
onto the hospice courtyard
and, from his bed,
he points to a camellia bush
heavy with red blossoms.

That's going to be my barometer, he says.
I'll look at it to see which way
the wind's blowing.
I saw those flowers turn their heads
into the sun this morning.
Now they've turned their backs on me.

He watches the bush,
the blossoms, the breeze all day
and then, after supper,
which he does not eat,
he turns his back on the camellias
and they become
the last blooms he ever sees.

Graveyard

The summer grass is sown with bones:
dinosaurs and giant sloths,
Choctaw and Cherokee,
slain Civil War soldiers.

Loyal dogs are buried in backyards;
unfaithful cats go missing. Milk cows
lie down in green pastures;
black bears fall to the forest floor.

Mixed among them: my father's bones,
spotted and cracked with cancer;
my grandmother, bled dry
after the birth of my mother;
a fragmented cousin returned
in a body bag from Vietnam.

The facts are non-negotiable.
Even if you mean no harm,
a gritty wind blows over the earth,
raps and riddles your shoulders.

The half-moon is a headstone lodged
in the infinite throat of the night.

Back to the River

Everywhere I look
there is work to be done:
the feeding of the poor,
the rescue of damaged children,
a need to understand
the diminishment of the aged.
There are also the dishes,
smeared with remnants of rich stew,
clumps of yellow daylilies
in want of division,
windowpanes perpetually smudged
because a resolute cardinal
keeps pecking to come in.
When I walk along the river,
I note with envy
the grace of the great blue heron,
which opens its wide wings
and sails across the water,
steps delicately along the bank,
always seems to know
which way to turn.

Acknowledgments

I am grateful to the following journals and their editors for publishing my work, some in slightly different versions:

Curio Poetry: "Re-turning"
Flycatcher: "On the Brink," "Trespass"
Foundling Review: "Eggshell"
Heron Tree: "Order *Lepidoptera,* Family *Papilionoidea*"
James Dickey Review: "This Lonely Cognizance"
Loose Change Magazine: "Whereupon the Writer Thinks
    She Is the Center of the Universe"
The Penwood Review: "Good Friday, Tybee Island"
Slice of Life: "Coyote," "Back to the River" (as parts of a larger
    piece)
Split Rock Review: "Autobiography"
Southern Humanities Review: "Graveyard"
The Southern Women's Review: "Dogwood Winter"
STILL: The Journal: "Fluent in Rivers," "Sweater Weather"
Valparaiso Poetry Review: "Sapelo"
Yemassee: "The Husker"

My heartfelt gratitude goes to my encouraging, unvanquished mother, Norma Brewin Ward; my husband Jeff, for his pride in and enthusiasm for my writing; my incredibly talented daughter, Rosalee; and my son Ben, who inspires me every day. Thanks also to the Side Door Poets and Wright's Writers; Christopher Martin; Rochelle Hurt; Thomas Lux; Susan Laughter Meyers; FutureCycle editor extraordinaire Diane Kistner; and, for exceptional guidance, William Wright.

Cover artwork by Rosalee Lewis; author photo by Keiko Guest;
interior book design by Diane Kistner (dkistner@futurecycle.org);
Adobe Garamond Pro text with Brandon Grotesque titling

About FutureCycle Press

FutureCycle Press is dedicated to publishing lasting English-language poetry books, chapbooks, and anthologies in both print-on-demand and ebook formats. Founded in 2007 by long-time independent editor/publishers and partners Diane Kistner and Robert S. King, the press incorporated as a nonprofit in 2012. A number of our editors are distinguished poets and writers in their own right, and we have been actively involved in the small press movement going back to the early seventies.

The FutureCycle Poetry Book Prize and honorarium is awarded annually for the best full-length volume of poetry we publish in a calendar year. Introduced in 2013, our Good Works projects are anthologies devoted to issues of universal significance, with all proceeds donated to a related worthy cause. Our Selected Poems series highlights contemporary poets with a substantial body of work to their credit; with this series we strive to resurrect work that has had limited distribution and is now out of print.

We are dedicated to giving all of the authors we publish the care their work deserves, making our catalog of titles the most diverse and distinguished it can be, and paying forward any earnings to fund more great books.

We've learned a few things about independent publishing over the years. We've also evolved a unique, resilient publishing model that allows us to focus mainly on vetting and preserving for posterity the most books of exceptional quality without becoming overwhelmed with bookkeeping and mailing, fundraising activities, or taxing editorial and production "bubbles." To find out more about what we are doing, come see us at www.futurecycle.org.

www.ingramcontent.com/pod-product-compliance
Lightning Source LLC
Chambersburg PA
CBHW060043050426
42448CB00012B/3117